THE OCEAN FLOOR

Keith Lye

The Sea

Exploiting the Sea
Exploring the Sea
Food from the Sea
Life in the Sea
The Ocean Floor
Waves, Tides and Currents

Cover picture: An underwater photographer filming
marine life on the floor of the Red Sea.

Series editor: Philippa Smith
Designer: Derek Lee

First published in 1990 by
Wayland (Publishers) Ltd
61 Western Road, Hove
East Sussex BN3 1JD, England

British Library Cataloguing in Publication Data
Lye, Keith
The Ocean Floor.
1. Oceans. Bed. Geological features
I. Title II. Series
551.4608

ISBN 1 85210 879 7   01/92 NEL $14.51

Phototypeset by Rachel Gibbs, Wayland
Printed and bound in Italy
by LEGO S.p.A.,Vicenza

CONTENTS

The US submersible Alvin *has been used to explore the Mid-Atlantic Ridge. It can take a crew of three people to a depth of 4,000 m.*

THE HIDDEN DEPTHS

The oceans cover about 70 per cent of the Earth's surface. Although little was known until recently about the ocean floor, people have always been interested in the sea. Those who lived along coasts had to know about the offshore waters they fished, and the whereabouts of hidden reefs that could rip holes in their boats. However, early sailors kept close to land, imagining that the open sea was filled with danger.

Between the fifteenth and eighteenth centuries, explorers sailed around the world. They mapped the coasts of most of the world's continents but they had little interest in the oceans and little or no idea of the depth of the water beneath their sailing ships. In 1773, a British scientist, using a weight attached to a rope, measured a depth of 1,248 m between Iceland and Norway. This was a record until another sounding of about 1,830 m was made in the North Atlantic Ocean in 1818.

In December 1872, a converted wooden warship, HMS *Challenger*, began a 3-year voyage around the world. The team of scientists on

Scientific studies carried out on the voyage of HMS Challenger *in the 1870s began the modern study of the oceans.*

board made many discoveries. They found living creatures at every depth and recorded 4,717 previously unknown species. They also learned much about the oceanic waters, and the resources they contain.

To measure the depths of the oceans they used lead balls, weighing about 90 kg, attached to many kilometres of sounding line. Measuring depths in this way was slow and sometimes inaccurate, as the sounding line often continued to unreel after the lead ball had hit the sea-bed. The depths they recorded surprised them. Near the Mariana Islands in the western Pacific Ocean, they measured a depth of about 8,180 m, which is not much less than the height of Mount Everest above sea-level.

The *Challenger* expedition marked the beginning of the modern study of the oceans – the science of oceanography. But although a great deal was learnt about ocean wildlife, currents and climate, there was little new information about the sea-bed. Most people still thought of it as a vast, flat plain. All the major discoveries about the ocean floor have been made in this century, with the help of modern inventions such as echo-sounding equipment, deep-sea cameras and submersibles.

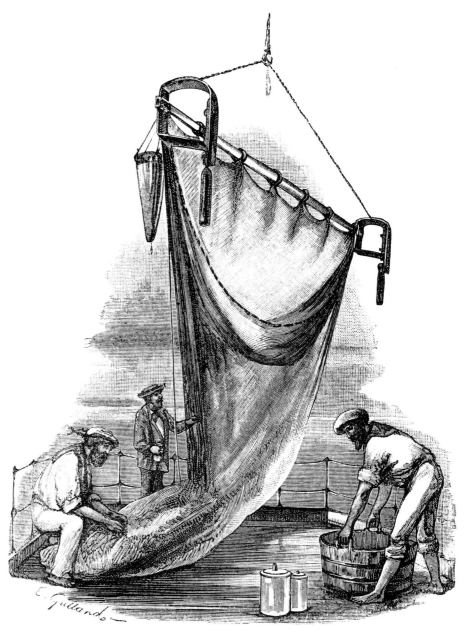

Above Scientists on board HMS Challenger *used large nets to obtain specimens during their round-the-world trip.*

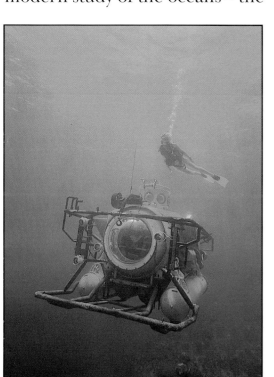

Left Divers now have many kinds of equipment to explore the ocean depths.

EXPLORING THE OCEAN DEPTHS

Echo-sounders were invented in the 1920s. Scientists had discovered that it is possible to measure the speed of sound through sea-water and that this speed never varies. An echo-sounder transmits sound waves through the water. The depth of water can be worked out by measuring the time it takes for the echo of the sound wave to bounce back from the sea-bed. Early echo-sounders could only measure short distances and were often unreliable, but improvements were made during the Second World War (1939–45) because of the need to pinpoint the positions of submerged enemy submarines.

Modern echo-sounders can take readings every second as a ship proceeds along a fixed course. Some echo-sounders are towed along the sea bottom or behind the ship. Some scan a wide area on either side of the ship's path. The signals are analyzed in a computer which produces a view of the sea-bed much like a strip of photographs of the ground taken from an aircraft. From the mass of data obtained by echo-sounders, the

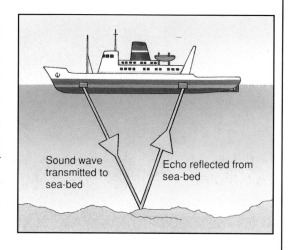

Sound wave transmitted to sea-bed

Echo reflected from sea-bed

Echo-sounders measure ocean depths by recording the time it takes for the echo of a sound wave to return from the ocean floor.

first accurate maps of the deep sea-bed were produced in the early 1970s.

Information about rock structures under the sea-bed, which is important when prospecting for minerals, comes from seismic techniques. These involve setting off explosions in the water and recording the shock waves reflected back by the rock layers below.

Deep-sea drilling is now important in oceanography. Between 1968 and 1983, a vessel called the *Glomar Challenger* sailed around the world, drilling hundreds of holes into the sea-bed. The cores of mud and bedrock that the drills brought to the surface gave clues to the origins of the oceans.

In the 1980s, a second ship, the *JOIDES Resolution*, took over the work. (JOIDES stands for Joint Oceanographic Institutions for Deep Earth Sampling.) This ship can work in depths of 8,300 m of water.

Other information about the sea-bed has come from descents in submersibles. The record descent was made by the bathyscaphe *Trieste*, which, in 1960, took Swiss scientist Jacques Piccard and Commander Don Walsh of the US Navy, down to a depth of 10,917 m in Challenger Deep in the Mariana Trench. In the 1970s, another submersible, the US *Alvin*, explored the Mid-Atlantic Ridge, an under-water mountain chain. Among its discoveries were hot springs rising from 'black smokers'. Black smokers are 'chimneys' made of minerals. They are formed when dissolved minerals, which rise up in the superheated water spurting

from the sea-bed, solidify in the cold ocean water. Some submersibles are not manned – instead they carry cameras and send back television pictures to the mother ship. In these and other ways, the mysteries of the oceans are gradually being solved.

A submersible is lowered into the sea.

Below The Gloria Deep Ocean Survey System can scan 60-kilometre-wide strips of the ocean floor. Measurements are used to make maps (*below left*).

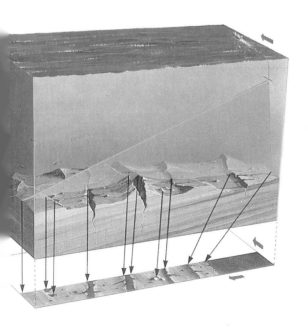

FEATURES OF THE OCEAN FLOOR

Until the 1930s nearly everyone believed that the sea-bed was mostly flat. But the scenery on the ocean floor is as varied as that on land.

Around most continents are shallow seas that cover gently sloping areas called continental shelves. These reach depths of about 200 m. Off some continents, the shelves are extremely narrow, but the average width is about 65 km. The surfaces of the continental shelves are uneven and covered by sand and mud. High areas form islands. During the last ice age, the shelves were mostly dry land and many of their features were moulded by glaciers and ice sheets. For example, many sand banks are made up of mud and rocks dumped there by ice sheets.

The continental shelves end at the steeper continental slopes which lead down to the deepest parts of the ocean. These slopes are the true edges of the continents. In places, the slopes are broken by gullies and deep canyons. Scientists think that these canyons may have been worn out by dense, muddy 'turbidity' currents, triggered off by earthquakes. These turbidity currents reach speeds of 50 to 80 kph, and they sweep sediment

The diagram below shows the main features found on the ocean floor.

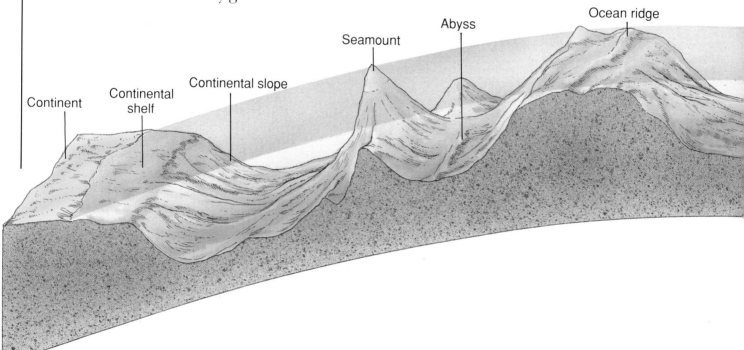

down the continental slopes where it piles up to form a gently sloping region called the continental rise.

Beyond the continental rise is the abyss. The abyss contains plains, long mountain ranges called ocean ridges, isolated mountains called seamounts, and ocean trenches, the deepest parts of the oceans. In the centres of some ocean ridges are long rift valleys, where earthquakes and volcanic eruptions are common. Some volcanoes that rise from the ridges appear above the surface as islands.

Other mountain ranges are made up of extinct volcanoes. Some seamounts, called guyots, are extinct volcanoes with flat tops. Scientists think that these underwater mountains were once islands but their tops were worn away by waves. Later, the sea-level rose and the sea-bed sank, submerging the seamounts. Some seamounts are capped by thick layers of coral.

Facts about the oceans

Area: About 362 million sq km, or nearly 71 per cent of the Earth's surface.

Average depth: 3,730 m.

Deepest point: 11,033 m in the Mariana Trench, in the western Pacific Ocean.

Mountains: The ocean ridges form a great mountain range, more than 64,000 km long, that weaves its way through all the major oceans. It is the largest single feature on Earth and covers about 23 per cent of its surface.

Highest mountain: Mauna Kea, Hawaii, USA, rises 10,203 m from its base on the ocean floor. Only 4,205 m are above sea-level.

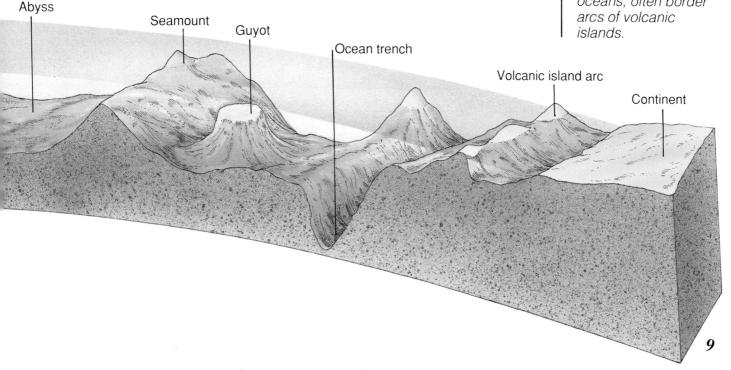

Ocean trenches, the deepest parts of the oceans, often border arcs of volcanic islands.

Abyss
Seamount
Guyot
Ocean trench
Volcanic island arc
Continent

THE CHANGING OCEANS

The cores of mud and rock brought back by deep-sea drilling ships vary greatly in age, but none of the rocks found in the crust under the oceans is more than about 200 million years old. This makes the oceans very young when compared with the continents, which contain rocks up to about 3,800 million years old. How then did the oceans form?

Before the First World War (1914–18) an American, Frank Taylor, and a German, Alfred Wegener, working independently, suggested that the continents had once been joined together, but that somehow they had split apart. Much evidence was collected to support this idea of 'continental drift'. First, the shapes of several land masses, such as South America and Africa, look as though they might once have fitted together, like pieces in a jigsaw. There are also similar rocks and rock structures along the edges of distant land masses, while fossils of the same ancient animals and plants are found in several widely separated continents. One way to explain this was continental drift, but no one could explain how continents could move.

Recent mapping of the ocean floor shows that the edges of the continental shelves along facing continents match up even better than the coastlines. Other evidence has come from magnetic studies. When new rock is formed from molten lava, magnetic minerals in the new rock are aligned with the Earth's magnetic field. But over the past several million years, the north and south magnetic poles have

About 200 million years ago, there was one huge land mass and one vast ocean.

been reversed many times. Bands of rock on either side of, and parallel to, the ocean ridges were found to be magnetized in reverse directions. Also, the youngest rocks are found in the centre of the ocean ridges. Away from the ridges, in both directions, the rocks become older and older. All these facts suggest that new rock is constantly being formed along the ridges and it is then being pushed away from the centre.

This and other evidence led scientists to believe in the theory of continental drift. In the late 1960s, a new idea, called plate tectonics, was born. This suggests that the Earth's outer layers are split into large, solid blocks called 'plates'. These plates are being moved by currents in the molten layer beneath.

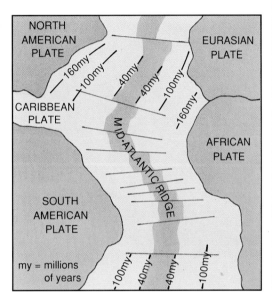

Left The youngest rocks on the ocean floor are in the ocean ridges. The oldest rocks are near the continents.

The map below shows the main plates which form the Earth's hard outer layers.

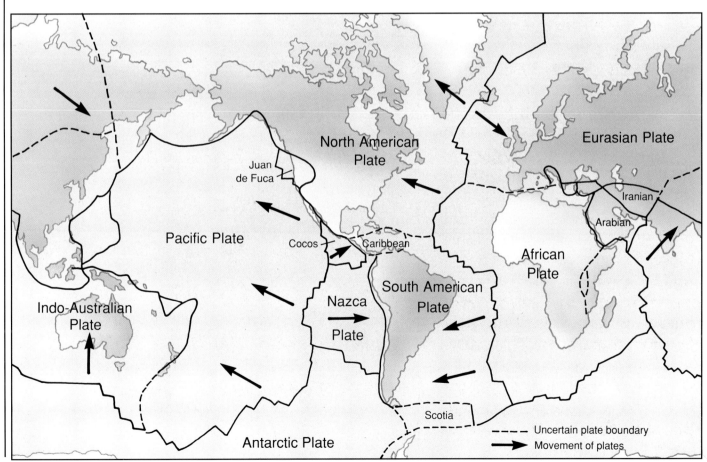

THE BIRTH OF AN OCEAN

The Earth's hard, outer shell is called the lithosphere. It consists of the crust, together with the top part of the mantle that underlies the crust. The lithosphere, which averages about 75 km in thickness, is split into seven large and several small plates. Beneath the lithosphere is a layer called the asthenosphere. Here the rocks are molten because of the great pressure and high temperatures. These hot, molten rocks, like other heated fluids, move around in 'convection currents'.

The rift valleys that run through the long ocean ridges are the edges between plates. The rocks in these valleys are hotter than elsewhere in the oceans. This is because molten material, or magma, is rising beneath them. Most of this magma spreads out sideways beneath the plates, forming sluggish currents that, like giant conveyor belts, pull the overlying plates apart. As the plates move apart, rising magma reaches the surface and fills the gap, creating new crustal rock. The plate movements fracture the rocks in the ocean floor, creating long breaks called 'transform faults' that lie roughly at right angles to the ridges.

1. Continents split along rift valleys

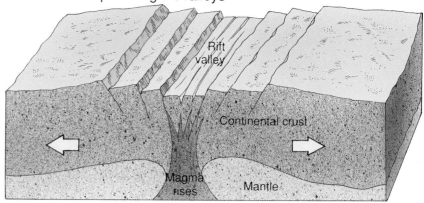

2. Water fills widened valley

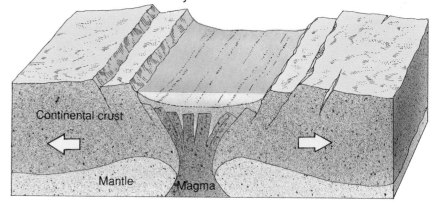

3. Ocean basin continues to widen

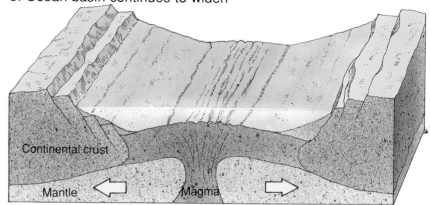

Land masses break apart along rift valleys. The rift valleys grow wider until they become ocean basins.

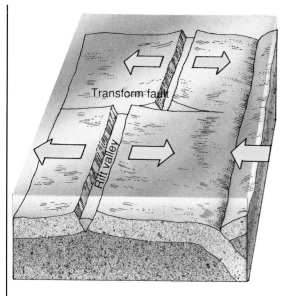

Transform fault

Rift valley

destroyed. This happens along the deep ocean trenches, where the liquid magma flowing beneath the plates cools and starts to sink. The overlying plate pushes against another plate and is forced down beneath it. This region is called a subduction zone. As the plate descends deep into the mantle, it melts. Sometimes some of this molten material returns to the surface through volcanic eruptions.

Left Transform faults are cracks formed when the Earth's plates move apart.

Below Where two ocean plates collide, one plate descends beneath the other and melts. Magma rises through volcanic islands. When a plate descends beneath a continent, the magma rises through volcanoes on land.

The movement of the plates on either side of the rift valleys is called sea-floor spreading and has created the world's ocean basins. Many ocean basins probably began as rift valleys on land. The currents in the magma below the Earth's crust gradually widened the rift valley, pulling it apart. Eventually, the sea flooded into the widening gap.

Sea-floor spreading is a slow process, taking between 1 and 10 cm a year. But over millions of years it can tear continents apart and create huge ocean basins. Certain features at the edges of South America and Africa, bordering the Atlantic Ocean, led scientists to suggest that these zones were once the edges of rift valleys, and that the two continents were once joined together.

While new crustal rock is being formed along the ocean ridges, elsewhere plates are being

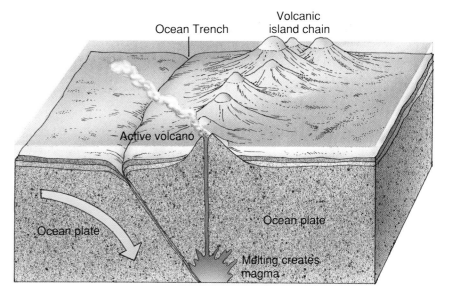

Ocean Trench

Volcanic island chain

Active volcano

Ocean plate

Ocean plate

Melting creates magma

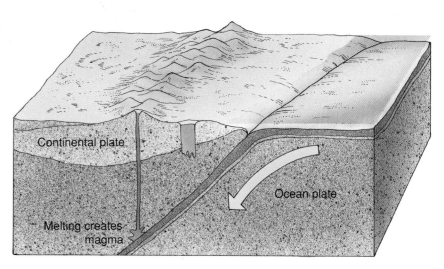

Continental plate

Ocean plate

Melting creates magma

6

THE RESTLESS OCEANS

Plate movements cause most volcanic eruptions and severe earthquakes. Probably more than half of the eruptions that take place every year are in the oceans, though few of them are recorded. Many volcanic seamounts rise from the ocean floor, and some of them appear as volcanic islands. Some volcanic islands occur in island arcs, alongside the trenches where one ocean plate is descending beneath another. The lava that reaches the surface in island arcs is formed by the melting of the descending plate. For example, the Mariana Islands, which lie near the world's deepest trench, in the west-central Pacific Ocean, and the islands of Japan, were all formed in this way.

In some places, such as off the west coast of South America, an ocean plate is descending beneath a continental plate. The molten rock from the melting plate rises through the overlying land mass and erupts through volcanoes in the Andes Mountains. Other volcanoes rise from the ocean ridges.

Some volcanic islands, such as the Hawaiian chain in the North Pacific Ocean, lie far from plate edges. Geologists (scientists who study rocks) think that these islands were formed as the Pacific Plate moved over a 'hot spot', a source of great heat in the Earth's mantle.

Many volcanic seamounts are capped by coral, a hard substance made by small, jelly-like creatures called coral polyps, which live in warm, shallow, clear water. But some coral islands are more than 1,000 m thick. Geologists believe that such great depths of coral can build up only if the sea-level changes or if the seamount sinks as a result of the sinking ocean plate.

Many volcanoes lie close to the edges of plates. A few lie above hot spots in the Earth's mantle.

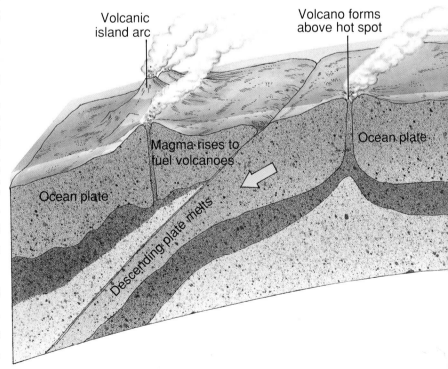

Plate edges, including ocean ridges, the deep trenches, and transform faults, where plates move alongside each other, are zones where earthquakes are common. Violent earthquakes occur when the edges of plates become jammed together. Pressure then builds up until the rocks break and the plates suddenly lurch forward.

Earthquakes and volcanic eruptions on the ocean floor trigger off tsunamis, which are fast-moving, destructive waves. These waves are often unnoticeable when in mid-ocean, but near land they increase in height as they slow down in shallow water. They often reach the shore as towering waves, many metres high, causing great destruction and loss of life.

Above White Island, a volcanic island off the coast of North Island, New Zealand, lies close to a plate edge.

Left Coral forms in warm, shallow seas. The coral polyps build up thick layers of limestone.

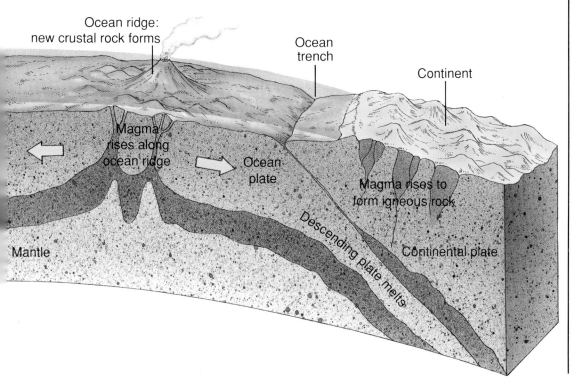

Ocean ridge: new crustal rock forms

Ocean trench

Continent

Magma rises along ocean ridge

Ocean plate

Magma rises to form igneous rock

Descending plate melts

Continental plate

Mantle

THE STORY OF THE OCEANS

The face of planet Earth is always changing. About 420 million years ago, a visitor from outer space would have seen four separate land masses surrounded by ancient oceans. The land masses were part of what is now North America; part of Europe; part of Asia, which geologists call Angara; and Gondwanaland, which consisted of what are now the southern continents of South America, Africa, Australia and Antarctica.

These land masses were on the move. First, plates bearing North America and Europe collided and the two formed Euramerica. About 275 million years ago, Euramerica and Angara collided to form an even bigger continent, Laurasia. Laurasia then became joined to Gondwanaland, and a single supercontinent, called Pangaea, was created. Pangaea was surrounded by Panthalassa, a vast ocean that is the ancestor of the Pacific.

Eventually, Pangaea began to break up. The oldest rocks on the floor of the North Atlantic Ocean are not much more than about 160 million years old, and it is thought that this was the time

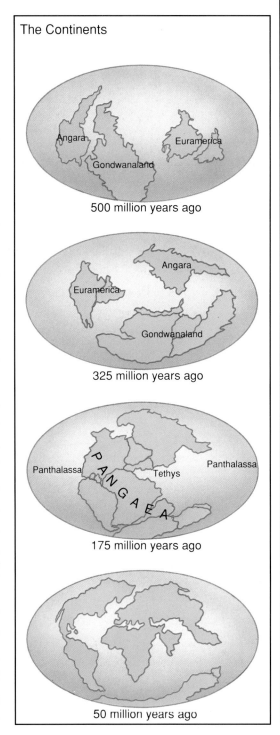

The Continents

500 million years ago

325 million years ago

175 million years ago

50 million years ago

These maps show how the continents have moved around over millions of years. Oceans have been created and then destroyed.

when North America began to move away from Europe. The South Atlantic Ocean started to open up 20 million years later, when South America began to move away from Africa. The break-up of Gondwanaland has continued throughout the last 100 million years.

The Atlantic, Indian and Pacific oceans were in existence by about 50 million years ago. In the Indian Ocean, a plate supporting India, which had once been joined to Africa, pushed against Asia. This plate collision squeezed up the sediments on the floor of the ancient Tethys Ocean into huge folds. These folded rocks now form the Himalayas. The Tethys Ocean, which once lay between Gondwanaland and Laurasia, has largely disappeared, but mountaineers who climb Mount Everest are treading on its remains.

The world map continues to change. If the Atlantic and Indian oceans continue to expand because of sea-floor spreading, then the Pacific Ocean will become much smaller than it is today. Another likely change in 50 million years' time is the gradual disappearance of the Mediterranean Sea – the last remnant of Tethys Ocean – caused by the northward movement of Africa against Europe. The Red Sea, which is

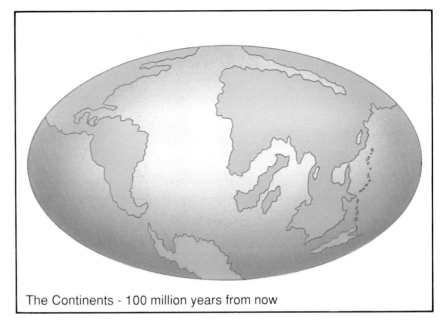

The Continents - 100 million years from now

now being widened by sea-floor spreading, is pushing the Arabian peninsula north-eastwards. This will eventually close up the Persian (or Arabian) Gulf. The sediments on the floor of the Gulf will be folded up into a new mountain range.

Above Over the next 100 million years, plate movements may make the world map look like this.

Below Africa is splitting apart along the East African Rift Valley.

OOZES

When scientists were dredging up samples from the rift valleys in the centres of the ocean ridges, they were surprised to find little or none of the muddy sediments, or oozes, that blanket most of the ocean floor. Instead, they hauled up newly-formed volcanic rocks. These rocks were made of lava that had been erupted on to the ocean floor, where it cooled quickly into rounded lumps covered with a glassy skin.

Geologists call this pillow lava. The discovery of these rocks and the absence of sediments showed that the rift valleys were extremely young parts of the ocean floor.

Terrigenous oozes cover about a quarter of the ocean floor. They are made up of material worn from the land by running water, glaciers and winds, and also ash erupted from exploding volcanoes. These oozes cover the continental shelves, slopes and

The map shows the various oozes that cover the ocean floor.

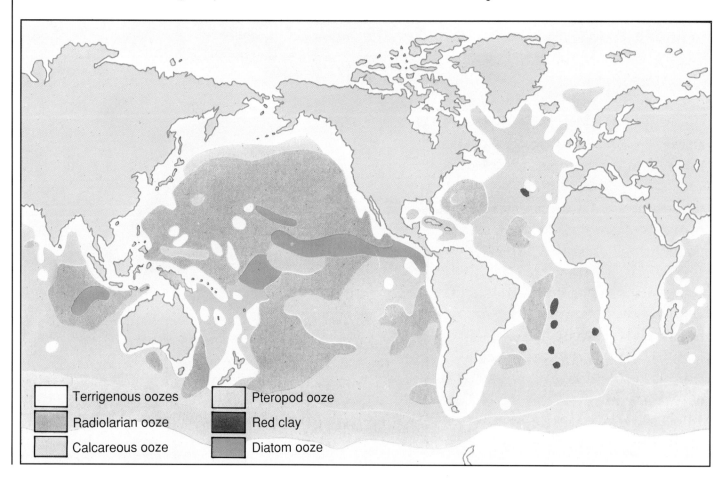

Terrigenous oozes

Radiolarian ooze

Calcareous ooze

Pteropod ooze

Red clay

Diatom ooze

the continental rises, and may be many kilometres thick. The coarsest material is usually found near land, while ocean currents sweep fine particles farther out to sea. Some of the thickest layers are found opposite the outlets of great rivers. Here, the sediments may build up at rates of several metres every 1,000 years. Some terrigenous oozes also occur on deep-sea floors. They are mainly clays and muds, usually brown or red in colour, formed from dust that comes from the air. These deposits form slowly. It takes at least 1,000 years for a one-millimetre layer to form.

Other deep-sea sediments are composed largely of the remains of plants, shells, bones and teeth. They are called biogenic oozes. The most common consist mainly of calcite, the mineral that makes up limestone rocks. Some of these calcareous oozes are formed from the remains of tiny, single-celled animals called foraminifera. Others contain the remains of one-celled algae called coccoliths, or the shells of pteropods (floating snails). Calcareous oozes do not occur in waters deeper than 4,500 m because deep-sea water, which is rich in carbon dioxide, dissolves calcite. Calcareous oozes cover about half of the deep-sea floor. They build up at the slow rates of between 1 and 4 cm every 1,000 years.

Other oozes are rich in silica. Siliceous muds are formed from diatoms (one-celled algae), and radiolaria (one-celled animals). Siliceous muds are common in parts of the Pacific Ocean where there is very little terrigenous sediment, and in the waters surrounding Antarctica.

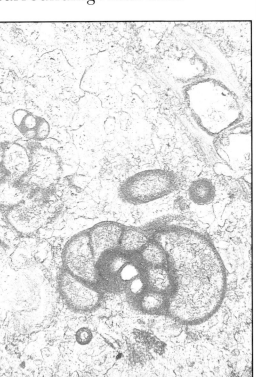

Above Some of the ash erupting from this volcanic island off Hawaii, USA, will settle on the ocean floor as terrigenous ooze.

The remains of tiny creatures called foraminifera form calcareous oozes on the deep-sea floor.

RESOURCES

Today, the main resources of the ocean floor are deposits of oil and natural gas found in the rocks beneath the continental shelves. Oil was first extracted from a well in offshore waters in 1896. At first this was a very expensive and dangerous operation, and even today, the cost of an offshore oil rig is about ten times more than that of a land rig. However, as land reserves of these fuels are used up, so the offshore deposits are becoming increasingly important.

The modern techniques of offshore oil drilling were first developed in the sheltered waters of Lake Maracaibo, a shallow sea inlet in Venezuela. From the early 1950s, drilling rigs were designed to operate in deeper water and harsher conditions, such as the stormy North Sea and the icy Canadian Arctic. Work on oil rigs remains dangerous. For example, an explosion and fire on a North Sea oil platform, 190 km north-east of Aberdeen, Scotland, killed 167 people in 1988.

Some minerals are found in the sediments in shallow coastal waters. Diamonds are mined in the gravel off the coast of Namibia in south-west Africa,

while tin ore occurs in the seas around Malaysia. Such deposits can usually be mined by dredging. Other metals are found on the deep-sea floor. The scientists on board HMS *Challenger* in the 1870s discovered that parts of the deep ocean floor, especially in the Pacific Ocean, contain vast numbers of roughly

Offshore oil rigs produce much of the world's oil supply.

Diamonds are found in the deposits along the shore of the African country of Namibia. The sea wall prevents flooding.

circular lumps of metal, called manganese nodules. These nodules, which measure between 0.5 and 25 cm across, contain not only manganese, but also iron, aluminium and magnesium, as well as some cobalt, copper, nickel and other metals in tiny quantities. Scientists do not fully understand how the nodules form. They seem to grow very slowly, layer by layer, from dissolved metals in the water.

Little interest was shown in the nodules until the late 1950s, when the high-quality land reserves of certain metals, including those in the nodules, began to be used up. But cheap ways of mining the nodules are needed. One idea is to use huge suction pipes to suck the nodules to the surface. But there is also a legal problem concerning ownership. Some countries argue that the oceans' resources should belong to everyone, not just to those that have the technology to make use of them.

Manganese nodules are potato-shaped lumps made up of several metals. The map shows how manganese nodules are scattered over large areas of the deep ocean floor.

Map to show areas of ocean floor with rich deposits of manganese nodules

KEY

▢ Manganese nodules

▣ Possible mining areas

THE PACIFIC OCEAN

The Pacific is the world's largest ocean, covering a greater area than all the continents put together. It is also the deepest ocean, with the greatest average depth. It contains the Mariana Trench, the deepest of all the ocean trenches. The Pacific is largely surrounded by an active zone where volcanic eruptions and severe earthquakes are common. The zone stretches from New Zealand round to southern Chile and is called the 'ring of fire'.

The floor of the Pacific Ocean is divided into several plates, the largest of which is the Pacific Plate. The Nazca and Cocos plates are bordered to the west by

The map shows the main features on the floor of the Pacific Ocean.

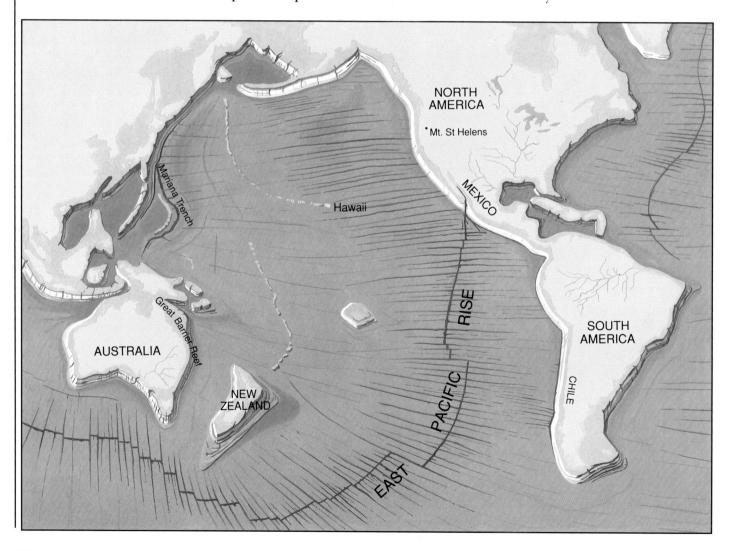

a ridge of mountains called the East Pacific Rise. Along this ocean ridge, sea-floor spreading is occurring at 8–10 cm a year, which is a faster rate than anywhere else in the world. Another feature of the eastern Pacific is a series of huge fractures (transform faults) running mainly from east to west.

The Nazca and Cocos plates are descending in subduction zones along deep trenches beneath the South American and Caribbean plates to the east. The descending plates melt and the molten rock fuels a chain of volcanoes running from Mexico, through Central America, to Chile. The Juan de Fuca Plate is descending beneath the North American Plate, fuelling volcanoes in the Cascades range, including Mount St Helens which erupted in 1980.

In the western Pacific Ocean, the Pacific Plate is descending along a series of deep trenches, under the large Eurasian and Indo-Australian plates. The east-central Pacific also includes the smaller Philippine Plate, which is almost entirely bounded by trenches.

The Pacific Ocean contains thousands of islands. Some are chains of volcanic islands bordering the trenches. There are also more than 10,000 volcanic mountains, including the Hawaiian islands, and many underwater seamounts that were formed over hot spots.

Manganese nodules are to be found south-east of Hawaii, and they may become an important source of metals in the future.

Many of the volcanic islands in the Pacific have slowly begun to sink and are covered with caps of coral. The living coral is at the surface, forming beautiful coral reefs. The largest reef in the world is the famous Great Barrier Reef, off the east coast of Australia, which stretches nearly 2,000 km.

Sea creatures in the Pacific's Mariana Trench, the deepest trench in the oceans.

Facts about the Pacific Ocean

Area:	165,200,000 sq km.
Average depth:	4,280 m.
Greatest depth:	11,033 m in the Mariana Trench.

The Great Barrier Reef is a large area of coral islands and reefs off the coast of Australia.

THE ATLANTIC OCEAN

The Atlantic is the second largest ocean. It is also the shallowest, partly because it has large areas of continental shelves, especially off North America, Europe and southern South America.

The most noticeable feature in the ocean's abyss is the S-shaped Atlantic Ridge, which runs the entire length of the ocean. Much of the ridge is between 2,100 and 3,000 m below sea-level. But the volcanic islands of Iceland, the Azores, Ascension Island and Tristan da Cunha are all parts of the ridge that appear above sea-level. A new land area rose from the ridge in 1963, when the volcanic island of Surtsey appeared off the coast of Iceland.

Along the centre of the ridge is a rift valley, between 24 and 48 km wide. Here volcanic action is common, because of the sea-floor spreading that is constantly widening the ocean. The rate of movement is quite slow, at about 2 cm a year. Other major features of the Atlantic Ridge are massive east-west fractures (transform faults) that cross it. Movements along these faults have displaced sections of the central rift valley.

Between the Atlantic Ridge and the continents are vast plains that end at the continental rises, where piles of sediments which have come mainly from the land, reach depths of more than 5 km. Above, the continental slopes are split by many deep canyons. The Atlantic has only two trenches. One is the South Sandwich Trench, which lies east of the Falkland Islands in the South Atlantic. The other is the Puerto Rico Trench, which forms the edge of the small Caribbean Plate. Along the trench, crustal rock from the floor of the Atlantic is being forced downwards and then melts. The magma formed in this way rises through volcanoes in the Lesser Antilles chain. One of the greatest eruptions in this chain occurred in 1902, when Mount Pelée, on Martinique, exploded with great force, killing 30,000 people.

Facts about the Atlantic Ocean

Area:	31,350,000 sq km.
Average depth:	3,330 m.
Greatest depth:	8,648 m in the Puerto Rico Trench.

Right The map shows the main features on the floor of the Atlantic Ocean.

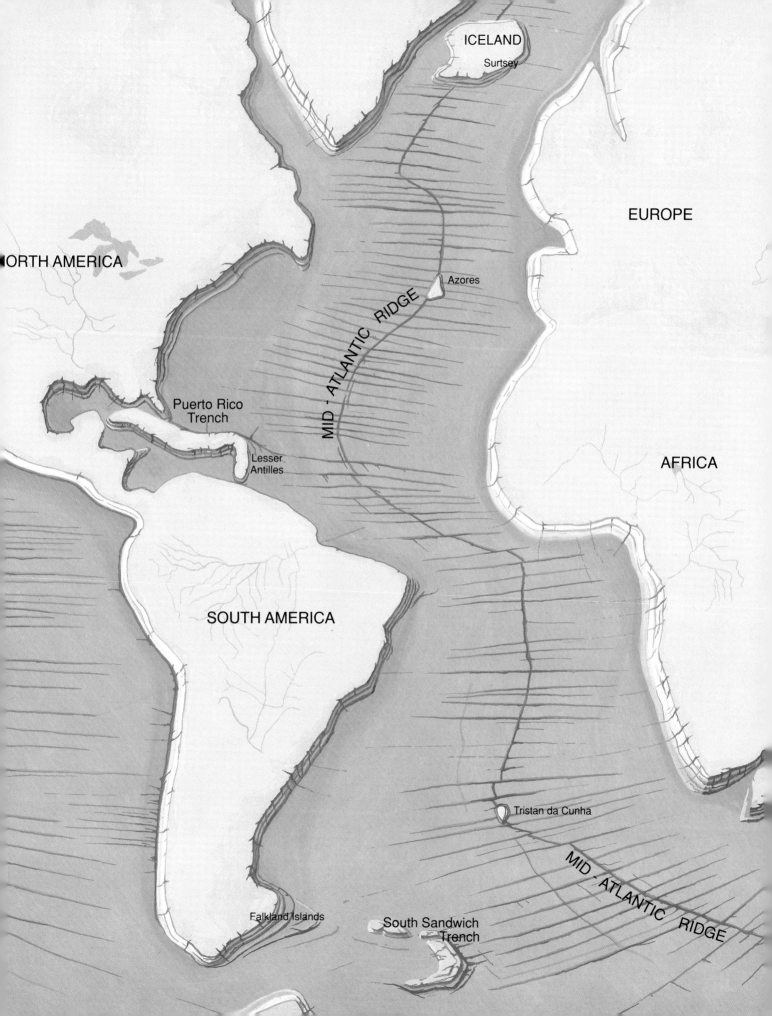

THE INDIAN OCEAN

The Indian Ocean lies mostly in the southern hemisphere between Africa, southern Asia, Australia and Antarctica. It was formed by sea-floor spreading as Gondwanaland broke up over the last 170 million years.

The ocean's main feature is a huge ridge, crossed by many long fractures. The ridge divides into two arms east of Madagascar. One arm runs around Africa and links up with the Atlantic Ridge. The other arm extends south of Australia and eventually links up with the East Pacific rise.

As in the other oceans, the central rift valleys in the ridges are zones where earthquakes and volcanic eruptions are common. Sea-floor spreading is gradually widening the ocean, pushing the Indo-Australian Plate north-eastwards and forcing it under the Eurasian Plate along the Java Trench, the only major trench in the Indian Ocean. North of the Java Trench lies a volcanic island chain which forms Indonesia. Indonesia has more active volcanoes than any other country.

In the north-east, the Indian Ocean Ridge is linked with a spreading ridge in the Rcd Sea. Sea-floor spreading, which has been occurring here for the last 25 million years, is gradually opening up the Red Sea and pushing Saudi Arabia north-eastwards.

The northern part of the Indian Ocean contains huge quantities of sediment from the land. One area, on the floor of the Arabian Sea, has been built up by material deposited by the Indus River. An even bigger volume of sediment has been dumped on the floor of the Bay of Bengal by the Ganges and Brahmaputra rivers. These areas of sediment, thousands of metres thick, are shaped like great fans.

The Indian Ocean contains many shallow, earthquake-free ridges and plateaux, which were

A diver photographs coral formations on the floor of the Red Sea, an arm of the Indian Ocean.

not created by sea-floor spreading. The ridges were probably formed, like the Hawaiian islands in the Pacific Ocean, as plates moved over a 'hot spot' in the mantle. The underwater plateaux are more difficult to explain. Some geologists think that they are the remains of continental land areas that have been moved by sea-floor spreading. As they moved, they gradually subsided into the ocean crust and sank beneath the waves.

Facts about the Indian Ocean	
Area:	73,600,000 sq km.
Average depth:	3,890 m.
Greatest depth:	7,450 m in the Java Trench.

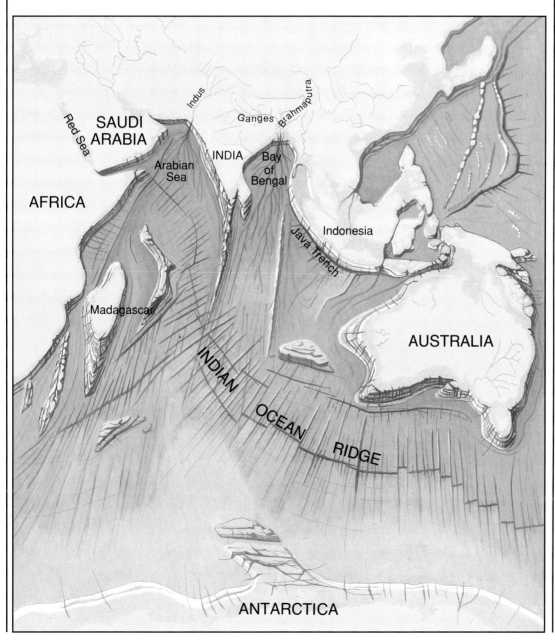

The map shows the main features on the floor of the Indian Ocean.

27

THE ARCTIC OCEAN

Some people believe that the waters around the North Pole are a part of the Atlantic, mainly because they are joined to the Atlantic Ocean by a broad stretch of sea between Scandinavia and Greenland. However, most oceanographers call these waters, much of which are covered by pack ice, the Arctic Ocean.

Continental shelves make up about one-third of the floor of the Arctic Ocean. Off the north coast of the USSR, the continental shelf is never less than 480 km wide and, in places, it is more than 1,600 km wide. Off the north coasts of Alaska and Canada, the shelves are much narrower, ranging between about 80 and 200 km wide. In recent years, geologists have been prospecting for oil and gas in these shallow seas.

The map shows the main features on the floor of the Arctic Ocean.

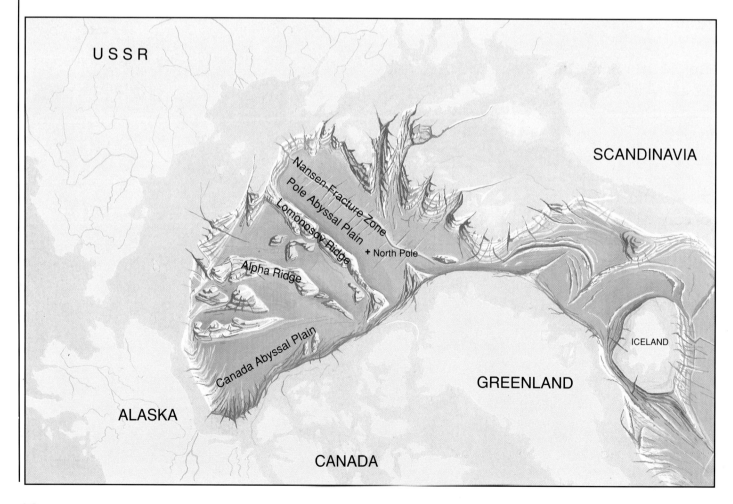

USSR

SCANDINAVIA

Nansen-Fracture Zone

Pole Abyssal Plain

Lomonosov Ridge

Alpha Ridge

+ North Pole

ICELAND

Canada Abyssal Plain

GREENLAND

ALASKA

CANADA

The centre of the Arctic Ocean consists of a huge ocean basin crossed by two narrow ridges. The Mid-Arctic Ocean Ridge is part of the world system of ridges where sea-floor spreading is taking place. It is linked to the Atlantic Ridge, but it is offset by a huge fracture, called the Nansen Fracture Zone. A very long earthquake belt stretches across the Arctic Ocean from the Mid-Atlantic Ridge to the USSR. Earthquakes along this ridge are common.

Between the Mid-Arctic Ocean Ridge and the huge Lomonosov Ridge is the Pole Abyssal Plain, which contains the deepest parts of the ocean near the North Pole. If you were to stand on the ice at the North Pole itself, the ocean floor would be over 4,000 m beneath you. The Lomonosov Ridge is a high underwater mountain chain, rising by an average of more than 3,000 m above the ocean floor. A third ocean ridge, the Alpha Ridge, is now inactive. Between the Alpha Ridge and the Canadian continental shelf is the Canada Abyssal Plain, the largest area of deep ocean floor in the Arctic.

Some mysteries still remain concerning the Arctic Ocean. The Siberian side is opening up because of sea-floor spreading, but at the same time the North American and Eurasian Plates are moving north. This means that the Arctic Ocean is gradually getting smaller. Yet geologists have not found any active subduction zones in the oceans.

Facts about the Arctic Ocean

Area:	12,173,000 sq km.
Average depth:	990 m.
Greatest depth:	About 4,600 m in the Pole Abyssal Plain.

Oilfields have been found under the continental shelf north of Alaska and Canada.

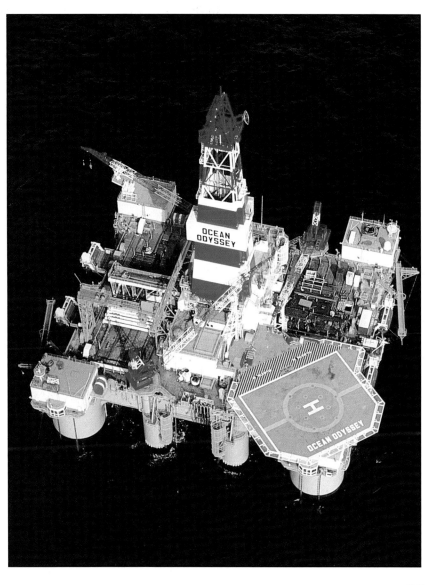

GLOSSARY

Algae Simple plants that live in oceans, in areas of fresh water or in moist soil. They include microscopic, one-celled plants and large, many-celled seaweeds.

Bathyscaphe An underwater vessel used for deep-sea research.

Bedrock The solid, unweathered rock that lies beneath the loose surface deposits of soil and mud.

Carbon dioxide A gas breathed out by animals and absorbed by plants. Water containing dissolved carbon dioxide reacts with and dissolves calcite, the mineral that makes up limestone.

Convection current When a gas or liquid is heated, particles near the heat source expand and rise. Near the surface, they cool and spread out. Finally the cool particles sink again and are reheated. This circulating movement is called a convection current.

Coral A limestone formation formed by tiny animals (coral polyps) that have hard limestone 'skeletons'.

Crust The outermost layer of the Earth. The continental crust reaches a thickness of 60–70 km under mountains. The oceanic crust averages only 6 km in thickness.

Currents Ocean currents are like giant rivers flowing through the sea, both near the surface and deep down. Currents of molten rock flow deep down below the Earth's crust.

Dredging Removing material from the bottom of a river, channel or the sea.

Extinct (of a volcano) Inactive; no longer liable to erupt.

Fault A fracture (or crack) in the Earth's crust, along which rocks move.

Fossils The remains of animals and plants that over millions of years have been converted into stone. They are usually found embedded in rocks.

Glacier A river of ice formed from snow. Glaciers carry rocks worn away from the land.

Gulley A small but deep channel.

Hot spot A place on the surface of the Earth beneath which hot rock is rising to the surface.

Hot spring A spring where hot water, usually heated by magma, reaches the Earth's surface.

Ice age An age in Earth history when ice spread over regions which now have warm or mild climates. During an ice age, the ice may advance and retreat many times, as the climate changes.

Ice sheet A vast, thick mass of ice, which covers large land areas in the polar regions.

Lava Molten rock (magma) that reaches the Earth's surface during volcanic eruptions.

Limestone A common rock formed on the beds of oceans. It consists mainly of the mineral calcite.

Magma Hot liquid rock below the Earth's surface.

Magnetic field The area of magnetic force around a magnet.

Magnetic poles Probably because of movements in the Earth's liquid outer core, which generate electricity, the Earth is like a giant magnet. As such, it has magnetic North and South Poles, which are located near the geographic poles. Periodically, the poles switch positions.

Mantle The part of the Earth between the crust and the core. It is about 2,600 km thick.

Minerals Solid, inorganic (lifeless) substances which have a definite chemical composition (unlike rocks), and definite physical and chemical properties.

Molten Melted.

Pack ice Large blocks of sea ice wedged together in a huge mass.

Plateaux Wide, mainly level areas of high land.

Prospecting Exploring a region for gold or other valuable minerals.

Reef A line of rocks near a coast which may be uncovered at low tide and covered at high tide.

Rift valley A valley formed when a block of land sinks between long faults in the Earth's crust.

Sediment A substance like mud or sand that has settled on the bottom of a sea, lake or river.

Silica A common substance consisting of the elements silicon and oxygen.

Sounding A measurement of the depth of water.

Species A group of animals that can breed together to produce young like themselves, which are also able to breed.

Subduction zone A zone where part of the Earth's crust is pushed down into the mantle.

Submersible A small manned or unmanned craft used in oceanographic research. Unlike submarines, submersibles keep much of their equipment outside the pressurized hull that holds the crew.

Subsidence The gradual sinking of land to a lower level as a result of earth movements.

Superheated water Water heated to a temperature above its boiling point without boiling occurring.

Transform faults *See* Faults.

Volcanic ash Very fine fragments of magma hurled into the air during volcanic eruptions.

BOOKS TO READ

Discovering the Sea by S. Smith (Longman,1982)

The Oceans by Martyn Bramwell (Franklin Watts, 1987)

Oceanography by Martyn Bramwell (Macdonald,1988)

Protecting the Oceans by John Baines (Wayland,1990)

Seas and Oceans by David Lambert (Wayland,1987)

Undersea Machines by R. J. Stephens (Franklin Watts, 1986)

Undersea Technology by Mark Lambert (Wayland,1990)

Under the Sea by Brian Williams (Kingfisher,1988)

The World's Oceans by Cass R. Sandak (Franklin Watts, 1988)

INDEX

Picture Acknowledgements

Bruce Coleman Ltd 5(bottom/M.Timothy O'Keefe), 17(Gerald Cubitt), 23(bottom/M.Timothy O'Keefe); GeoScience Features 19(bottom); Michael Holford Library 4, 5(top); The Hutchison Library 20; Marconi Underwater Systems 7(bottom); OSF 15(middle/Pam & Willy Kemp); Seaphot Limited/Planet Earth Pictures 3 (Richard Chesher), 7 (top/John Menzies), 21 (middle/Robert Hessler), 23 (top/Robert Hessler); Zefa 15 (top), 19 (top), 21(top), 26, 29, *cover*. The illustrations on pages 6, 8/9, 10, 11, 12, 13, 14/15, 16, 17, 18 and 21 are by Peter Bull. The maps on pages 22, 25, 27 and 28 are by John Kearns. Cover and title page artwork by John Yates.